Piccadilly Circus in London was a place where fun flourished alongside the seamier side of life, while servicemen and women gathered to spend what little leave they had.

THE HOME FRONT

Guy de la Bédoyère

A Shire book

Published in 2005 by Shire Publications Ltd,
Cromwell House, Church Street, Princes Risborough,
Buckinghamshire HP27 9AA, UK.
(Website: www.shirebooks.co.uk)

Copyright © 2005 by Guy de la Bédoyère.
First published 2002; reprinted 2005.
Shire Album 400. ISBN 0 7478 0528 8.
Guy de la Bédoyère is hereby identified as the author of
this work in accordance with Section 77 of the Copyright,
Designs and Patents Act 1988.

British Library Cataloguing in Publication Data:
De la Bédoyère, Guy
The home front. – (A Shire book; 400)
1. World War, 1939-1945 – Social aspects – Great Britain
2. Great Britain – History – George VI, 1936-1952
3. Great Britain – Social conditions – 20th century
I. Title
941'.084
ISBN 0 7478 0528 8

Cover: *Office workers struggle to get to work past the debris caused by a bomb that fell the night before.*

ACKNOWLEDGEMENTS
I thank Lyn and Michael Hymers for allowing me to photograph items in their personal
collection of Home Front memorabilia. I also thank Denis Brown and Sally Brooman for
letting me photograph some of their Home Front stock at 'Merlins', Four Ways, East Kirkby,
Spilsby, Lincolnshire PE23 4BY. Telephone: 01790 763229, email: Merlins@silksheen.fsnet.co.uk
Website: www.merlins.flyer.co.uk

Printed in Malta by Gutenberg Press Limited, Gudja Road,
Tarxien PLA 19, Malta.

CONTENTS

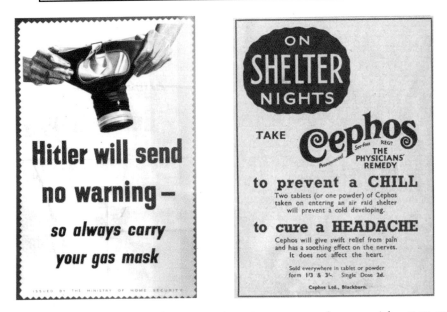

The war was an enormous publicity campaign. Government and commercial posters and advertisements reminded everyone that the war affected everything.

INTRODUCTION

The Home Front has been a part of conflict ever since wars began. Generations of British women and children learned to fend for themselves in the Middle Ages, and during the naval wars of the seventeenth, eighteenth and nineteenth centuries. But these were times when the people at home generally experienced the conflict at second hand. Shortages and crippled veterans aside, the violence of the wars passed them by.

Among the grimmest legacies of the twentieth century are the aerial bombardment of civilians, and submarine warfare. During the First World War, about 1400 people were killed in Britain by aerial bombs. New international economies meant that Britain became (and remains) hugely dependent on imports. Submarine development in the First World War was devastating. A single machine, unseen and unheard, could wreak havoc without warning, killing not only civilian passengers but sending vital cargoes to the bottom of the Atlantic. The sinking of the *Lusitania* off Ireland in 1915 was a body-blow, which exposed Britain's susceptibility to the new warfare.

The greatest threat to the Home Front came from the German U-boats. Here a U-boat crew mans the deck gun while a hapless merchantman sits in the distance.

Although the Junkers Ju87 'Stuka' dive-bomber was abandoned for use over England after August 1940, it remains a symbol of the terror of aerial bombardment. A special device produced an ear-splitting scream as it dived at targets.

When the Second World War broke out in 1939, plans were already afoot to create a Home Front. After 1918, a new philosophy of war had developed, based on the maxim that 'the bomber will always get through' (Stanley Baldwin, 1932). There was a climate of very genuine terror throughout Europe. The bombing of Shanghai by Japan in 1932 and the havoc wrought on Guernica and Barcelona in the Spanish Civil War made the prospects seem horribly vivid. The abrupt collapse of Poland in 1939 and of France in 1940 confirmed the fears.

The Home Front grew out of a need not only to protect the public but also to create the impression of protection. Britain's resources were going to have to be conserved, which meant doing without and making the best of what there was to go round. The Second World War was also the greatest mechanised war in the world's history. By far and away the largest proportion of the population remained in Britain throughout the war. In the end, the Home Front was about motivating these people, protecting them and encouraging them.

The Home Front was also about control. The British people experienced unprecedented Government intervention. Every aspect of daily life was regulated – from free speech to toilet paper. Government information, instructions and invectives poured into letter-boxes. Many pleasures in life disappeared – the seaside was out of bounds, fledgling television ceased for the duration, and some fruits and vegetables became distant memories.

All this was conducted in an environment where a bomb crashing through the roof could wipe out a

Bringing the nation together. This book cover presents a united nation in the face of war.

5

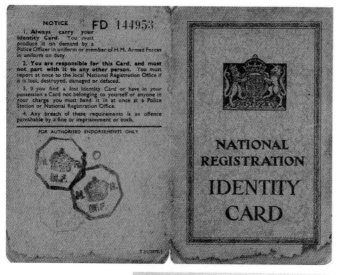

The standard national identity card, which might need to be produced at a moment's notice.

Some of the Government public-information leaflets distributed before and during the outbreak of war, advising on every possible aspect of life.

This advertisement for a series of encyclopaedias offered the customer the reassurance that his or her death from enemy action would not leave anyone liable for money still owing.

family in an instant. But there remained an underlying sense of purpose. The blatant dishonesty of the black market, and criminal gangs who stole ration coupons, clothing and food, added a *frisson* of excitement. Even so, it is easy uncritically to idealise the period in hindsight. The truth is that rationing, the black-out and the hedonistic sense that life could end in an instant also

The gas mask, carried every-where by everyone but never needed, has become the eternal symbol of the Home Front. This surviving example still has its canvas bag, and a capsule with a de-misting substance for the eye-glass. This example is dated December 1939.

contributed to a rise in crime and prostitution, ranging from casual indulgence in the black market to removing valuables from the bodies of people killed in the Blitz. Very few people could say that they took no part in this other side to the Home Front. The chance to buy an illicit luxury on the black market was hard to resist, especially after years of doing without. But minor infringements were often overlooked in the face of an overwhelming deter-mination to win the war.

The sense of purpose has subsisted in modern folk myth – today, anyone showing fortitude in the face of a flood or a gas explosion is said to have 'the Blitz spirit'. In every sense the best of times and the worst of times, the Home Front is still with us in a myriad of places around Britain. From the forgotten gas mask hanging under the stairs to the fading pamphlets in drawers and corroded air-raid shelters in the gardens, these all mark the time when, along with the rest of Europe, North Africa, the Pacific and Atlantic Oceans, the beaches of Normandy and the jungles of the Far East, every home across Britain stared war in the face.

St Paul's Cathedral, London. The cathedral's survival of the Blitz is commemorated today by a statue group of firemen.

Balham High Road in south London shows the effects of blast after a raid on 14th October 1940. The street frontage has been blown away by the bomb, which caused the crater where the bus is lying.

SECURING THE HOME

War brought the Government a very specific problem. It was essential that the workforce be kept close to places of work, and *at* work. This would guarantee that the production of munitions and military equipment, and the normal services of government and life, were maintained. The practical side is obvious, but there was also morale to consider. European images of refugees struggling along with carts had to be avoided in Britain.

Converting the proverbial Englishman's metaphorical castle into something approaching an actual fortress became a priority, even though when the war began in 1939 there were very real fears that millions of people were soon going to be killed by bombs. Trying to resist a direct hit was fairly futile, but some of the greatest damage caused by a bomb was from blast and fire. Blast involved a pulsating air wave, like the ripples from a stone dropped in a pond, expanding outwards from the point of impact. The rapid changes in air pressure could cause the entire façade of a building to blow outwards. The inhabitants fell out of or through the tumbling masonry, while passers-by were showered with debris.

Preparations for the Home Front were underway long before the declaration of war in September 1939. Issuing a pamphlet in early 1939 advising people on domestic defence, Wing Commander E. J.

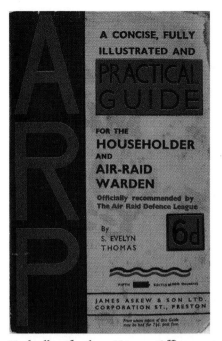

A CONCISE, FULLY
ILLUSTRATED AND

PRACTICAL
GUIDE

FOR THE
HOUSEHOLDER
AND
AIR-RAID
WARDEN

Officially recommended by
The Air Raid Defence League

By
S. EVELYN
THOMAS

6d

FIFTH ____ EDITION

JAMES ASKEW & SON LTD.
CORPORATION ST., PRESTON

From whom copies of this Guide
may be had for 7½d. post free.

This handy booklet contained reams of guidance on securing the house and building shelters.

A pictorial guide to dealing with bombs from the ARP booklet illustrated above.

Hodsoll of the Home Office was unequivocal in his warning that 'in the future, our security as a nation may depend on the security of the home'. One of the first precautions was obscuring houses from the air. As early as July 1939, a trial black-out run was ordered across the country, and air-raid exercises were conducted in many towns. Pamphlets offering guidance 'if war should come' were published, and manufacture began of items such as gas masks.

Advice was almost unlimited. The suggested 'refuge room' was a room set aside for specific reinforcement against the effects of blast and splintering. The idea was that it would withstand rather more knocks than the rest of the house and needed to have as few doors and windows as possible. A cellar might seem the obvious solution but not all houses had them, and in any case they were susceptible to flooding from blown-up water mains and to being completely blocked by falling debris. Large timbers were supposed to be laid across the floor, supporting timber braces to hold up the ceiling. A blanket

over the door, and rags or wet paper across windows and chimneys, would resist the ingress of poison gas – never used, but fear that it might be prevailed throughout the conflict – while sandbags or boxes of earth would buffer the windows, the glass being secured by strips of gummed paper.

With ominous rumblings of war about, some homeowners had already taken precautions long before 1939 by erecting purpose-built shelters. Many of these were ad-hoc arrangements and took the form of free-standing concrete blockhouses, or subterranean rooms reached by a flight of steps. The Government produced the Anderson shelter, a prefabricated corrugated-steel structure, designed for DIY erection in a specially dug hole in the

A delivery of prefabricated Anderson shelter components in a suburban street.

The theory: a family goes to bed under the Morrison shelter frame.

garden. It was supposed to accommodate four to six people. Many will recall Andersons, named after Sir John Anderson, Home Secretary and Minister of Home Security in 1939, as long-lasting post-war playhouses (indeed the Government even promoted them on the basis of their peacetime reuse as bicycle sheds). Their provision was in deadly earnest and the less well-off were provided with them free.

The practice: rescuers scramble in the wreckage of a house. Although battered, the Morrison shelter has survived better than the masonry.

The Anderson shelter saved numerous lives but it was cramped, cold and damp. For those who either would not or could not have an Anderson, the Government also distributed the Morrison shelter from 1941. Named after Herbert Morrison, Minister of Home Security, the Morrison was a steel frame, big enough for several people to lie under but small enough to serve as a table of sorts. It was supposed to be strong enough to be able to support piles of fallen masonry, which up to a point it did.

Public shelters existed for places where there were no gardens, but in London one of the most popular refuges was the underground railway system, though more affluent people repaired to basements in clubs and hotels. Others took a more fatalistic approach and stayed in pubs and cinemas. Public shelters did not appeal to everyone. They were not even necessarily safe. In March 1943, an accident on the stairs at Bethnal Green station led to 173 people being crushed or suffocated to death in the stampede.

One way of passing a night was a Blitz-themed set of jigsaw puzzles.

Householders were encouraged to keep their gas masks handy at all times and to prepare themselves with other gear. A stirrup-pump for putting out fires was recommended, as well as scoops and buckets of sand for dealing with incendiary bombs. Books, games and toys to keep children entertained during hours of air raids had to be gathered up and kept ready. Enterprising manufacturers serviced this new market.

Contemporary accounts and memoirs recall a world of patience and panic in blinding darkness as parents grabbed sleeping children, or when elderly people, confused by the howls of sirens, staggered out into the night waving torches to hunt for the enemy. The night passed in a mixture of fitful sleep, fractious children, and squabbles over games, cards and other entertainments pursued in the gloom.

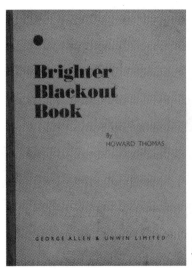

Black-outs caused chaos without any help from the Luftwaffe. Cars collided or lurched on to pavements, while pedestrians tripped down cellar steps or over paving-stones. Minor misdemeanours were seized on by zealous wardens, delighting in their new-found uniformed authority. A single lighted match – obviously invisible to a bomber overhead – could land the miscreant with a hefty fine. Meanwhile, crooks revelled in the opportunities to break into shops and warehouses with virtual impunity in the pitch-darkness, some even impersonating

An enterprising publisher produced this compendium of games and activities for filling out the night hours in an air-raid shelter.

Above left: *This axe, dated 1941, is of the type issued to ARP (Air Raid Precautions) wardens and firemen. It was used by Mr A. V. Braygar, who worked as a fireman during the Blitz in London and Orpington, Kent.*

Above right: *The silver badge worn by ARP wardens. This example is hallmarked for 1939.*

wardens and obtaining innocent police assistance in loading their getaway vans.

The morning meant a be-draggled return to normality, or to the traumatic discovery that the house was in ruins, or that a family member had been killed, leading a few days later to a terse note from the local authority permitting collection of the body for burial. For those who ex-perienced a direct hit and sur-vived, the horror was waking up hours later, pinned down by rubble, to the frantic efforts of shocked rescuers. Usually unable

An ARP warden at his sandbagged post. The sign 'Hotel Ritz' is an attempt at lightening the mood.

13

Cert. No. W / D._____

Register Ref._____

County Borough of Eastbourne
Name of Local Authority.

AUTHORITY TO REMOVE BODY.

To _Mrs Kay Hutchinson_

9. Hampden Avenue

Hampden Park

I, the undersigned, HEREBY CERTIFY that the death of _Sydney_

Alfred Hutchinson, Transport Driver

of _9 Hampden Avenue, Hampden Park, Eastbourne_

which occurred on _11th October 1940_ was due to

War Operations and I HEREBY AUTHORISE you to remove and dispose of [his] [her]

body at present resting in the Mortuary at _Police Headquarters, Eastbourne_

DATED this _14th_ day of _October_ 19_40_

_____

_____ Clerk of the Council.

NOTE.—This Certificate must be produced to the Mortuary Superintendent when application is made for removal of the body, and to the Undertaker when making arrangements for burial. Steps should not be taken to register the death of the deceased with the Registrar of Births and Deaths.

E.W.26. 5. Bennetts Bros. Ltd., London-m.

This terse note authorises collection of the body of a man killed in an air raid in Eastbourne, Sussex, on 11th October 1940.

to remember the raid, such bomb victims then had to come to terms with the loss of perhaps their entire families.

Looting was widespread, with crooks, public officials and passers-by among the culprits. When a family survived the night only to find that their home was wrecked beyond repair, the trauma of lost possessions was overtaken by the need to find new accommodation. Rest centres (often schools) provided an inadequate first stop, while Government compensation was supposed to make good the losses. But the process was agonisingly slow. It was not until mid 1944 that the Government started to produce prefabricated houses in which bombed-out families could live.

Prime Minister Winston Churchill tours a bomb-torn area in Battersea, London, during September 1940. This show of solidarity was an essential part of bolstering the Home Front.

BOMBS

Dropped in colossal numbers, the incendiary (fire) bomb caused incalculable damage. A high-explosive bomb could demolish a house and its neighbours in an instant but the wreckage was generally restricted to the vicinity. The laying waste of large tracts of British cities testified to the effectiveness of incendiaries, weight for weight, some five times more effective than conventional explosives.

A triumphant article in 'War Illustrated' reassured its readers of the technical inferiority of German bombs.

The incendiary exploited magnesium's spectacular ability to burst into flames. The basic device weighed 1 kg or 2 kg (about 2 pounds or 4 pounds) and consisted of a cylinder of magnesium with a central core of thermite (a highly combustible compound of aluminium and iron oxide), fitted with a flush steel tail and an explosive device in the head. The explosive was intended merely to start a small fire, causing the magnesium and thermite, which burns at a temperature of around 3000°C (5432°F), to ignite. At this stage, they could be easily put out with a bucket of sand. But, once ignited, the bomb could burn for three to

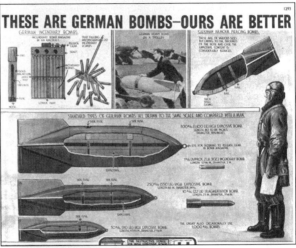

THESE ARE GERMAN BOMBS–OURS ARE BETTER

Far left: *How to dispose of an incendiary: grip it by the steel tail and hurl it from the roof into the garden, or douse it with a bucket of sand.*

Left: *The incendiary on the left fell on West Malling airfield, Kent, in August 1940 but failed to ignite. The one on the right fell on a factory in Sidcup, Kent, and helped set fire to the building, leaving just the scorched steel tail.*

St Michael's Cathedral, Coventry, smoulders after incendiaries destroyed it on the night of 14th/15th November 1940.

four minutes. Unattended, this was time enough to utilise the potential energy in the materials that went to make up a building, often by setting wooden rafters or furniture alight. In the terror, it was not unknown for fire wardens to flee for shelter, abandoning their posts. Today, there is no more potent memorial to incendiaries than the ruins of Coventry Cathedral.

Fire was so effective that it is not surprising there were other methods of causing it. There were many variations on the incendiary, including more conventional-looking bombs with incendiary fillings such as an exceptionally unpleasant model called the *Phosphorbrandbombe*. Phosphorus formed part of the filling but was kept separate in glass containers. These shattered on impact, allowing the phosphorus to mix with oil and rubber in the rest of the casing. The resultant spreading and burning liquid could cause horrific injuries.

A German crew prepares a V1 flying bomb (called a 'doodlebug' in Britain) for launch towards its target.

Other bombs formed variants on basic high-explosive types and were known as SC bombs. Of various weights from 50 kg (1 cwt) to 2500 kg (about 2^1/$_2$ tons), these contained TNT and other explosives such as amatol (made of ammonium nitrate and trinitrotoluene). The Luftwaffe also dropped aerial mines and armour-piercing bombs, but these both were intended primarily for destroying enemy shipping or military fortifications. Mines were intended for shipping lanes but, being designed to explode on accidental impact with dry land (to prevent their mechanisms being dismantled for analysis), they could also cause major damage to buildings. This led to their intentional use on land-based targets during the Blitz with such devastating effect that immediate moves were made to censor any publicity about them.

Bombs had one advantage – there was normally a warning of enemy aircraft approaching. The coming of the V-weapons

A garden in Noble Street, in the City of London, preserves the remains of bombed-out buildings to this day, overlooked by the Barbican development. This part of the city would be unrecognisable to anyone from before 1940.

later in the war changed all that. The V1 was a cigar-shaped unmanned projectile with wings and a tail-unit, powered by a pulse-jet engine. Dispatched towards south-east England from secret silos, the V1 continued on its trajectory until the fuel ran out, marked by the characteristic abrupt end to the rattling burble of its engine noise – the only warning anyone got. Then it fell to earth, exploding on impact. During the summer of 1944, an average of over one hundred V1s per day caused devastation. The psychological damage was probably greater because the V1 could only be stopped by a high-speed fighter chase: the fighter pilot would catch up the V1 and use his wings to flip the projectile over, making it crash into the countryside.

The V2, however, was unstoppable and inaudible. Gradually supplanting the V1 from September 1944, the V2 was a supersonic missile, immune to Allied fighters and defences, reaching an altitude of 60 miles (96.5 km) and speeds in excess of 3500 mph (5631.5 km/h). More than 1100 fell on England, and they were undetectable until the explosion was heard. Even more terrifyingly, initially no one knew what was causing the damage and leaving craters more than 20 feet (7 metres) in diameter. The V2 had the capacity to wipe out a whole town block at once, killing dozens of people and trapping thousands more under rubble.

By the end of the war, a total of 60,595 civilians were recorded to have been killed by enemy action in Britain, just under half (29,890) of whom died in London. A further 86,182 were seriously injured. The September 2001 terrorist attacks on New York City and Washington resulted in a total number of deaths equivalent to about twelve per cent of London's losses over six years – in the space of two hours. Appalling though Britain's 1939–45 losses were, the figures were far lower than anyone had expected before war broke out. It was this that made it possible for the Home Front to function and not dissolve into panic.

On 8th September 1944, one of the first V2 rockets fell at Staveley Road, Chiswick, London, causing this memorable scene of devastation. In the foreground is the crater, but the blast has demolished numerous houses.

FOOD AND GARDENING

During the First World War, submarine warfare introduced Britain to food shortages, leading eventually to a rationing system. Britain's steady industrialisation and urbanisation in the nineteenth century had already led to dependence on imported foods. Around sixty per cent was imported in 1939; this even included something as banal as the onion. The fall of the Channel Islands in the early summer of 1940 brought to an end most of Britain's supplies of this unexpected casualty of the conflict.

In 1939 Britain had 21.6 million tonnes of merchant shipping afloat, targeted by Germany from the outset. The sinking of Germany's battleship *Bismarck* in 1941 brought to an end any serious attempt to use surface ships against the merchant fleets, with resources being concentrated thereafter in the submarines (U-boats). Until the cracking of ciphers used by the Germans, progress in radar and the arrival of long-range American B-24 Liberator aircraft for RAF Coastal Command, Britain's entire future started to look bleak as U-boats destroyed millions of tonnes of shipping and, with them, vast stocks of food and war matériel being brought from North America.

In 1937 the Ministry of Food was established as part of the preparations for the expected war so that rationing could be established from the outset, with separate divisions charged with responsibility for different categories of food. Planning was based on self-administering geographical regions, each of which operated through local food offices.

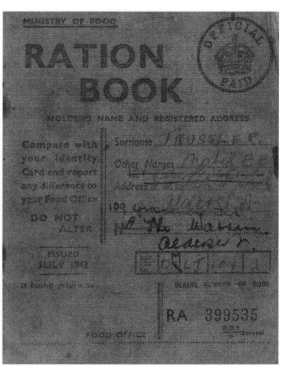

The principle was simple. An individual allowance of food was obtained with money and the relevant coupons. If a person's allowance had already been used, then it was illegal for the shopkeeper to sell him or her the product. This was recognised as being fair, even though wealthy people could purchase restricted goods on the black market. In rural areas, the issue was quite different. Local supplies of meat

Without this vital document, the owner was unable to buy rationed goods.

18

Some basic brand names, still familiar today, fortified their own image in the war.

MAKES COOKING SO EASY

were quite likely to increase suddenly with the slaughter of, for example, a pig, from which a whole village could benefit.

The underlying fairness of the rationing system meant that poorer people benefited. Official calculations of minimum nutritional requirements meant that some scarce foods like orange juice could be targeted, particularly at small children and pregnant women, rather than decorating an affluent breakfast table. Regulation of prices meant basic food remained affordable. The result was that pre-war levels of juvenile deaths, rickets and other developmental abnormalities dropped significantly. It was also easy for the Government to present rationing and economy as a moral issue. Posters exhorted the Home Front to do its 'job in the Battle of the Atlantic', pointing out that, while peacetime waste cost money, 'waste in war costs lives'.

In the home, this translated into making do with less and making other things do when the required food or substance was unavailable. Nothing could be more symbolic of wartime food economy and shortages than the dried egg, or more incomprehensible today in an age of factory farming that has made the fresh egg abundant and cheap. A daily radio programme extolled the virtues of preparing meals without meat, and other economies.

Queuing was an everyday experience for Britain's housewives. But the hours of patient waiting were often followed by disappointment. These ladies are armed with old newspaper for wrapping their purchases.

Just because food supply was regulated, having the money and coupons to pay for it did not guarantee availability. Queuing for hours in the cold became part of the daily routine, especially for the few kinds of goods, including fish and sausages, that had escaped rationing. The moment a fishmonger or butcher got hold of supplies, lines of resilient housewives formed outside his shop, regardless of the weather or even sometimes of air-raid warnings, with those at the back experiencing tearful frustration when the food ran out before they had a chance to buy anything. A three-hour wait for something as basic as three apples was the sort of inconvenience shoppers were prepared to tolerate. Queues formed for almost anything at all, with some of the most earnest being formed by pet-owners seeking food for their cats and dogs.

Kitchen equipment was spartan by today's standards, making it impossible to store fresh foods for more than a day or two. Refrigerators were rare, and most people had to depend on larders, and bowls of cold water to chill milk and butter. None of this was new, but in a time of shortage a jug of spoiled milk was a disaster, not an inconvenience. Similarly, the exhortations to contribute to 'Spitfire Funds' sent many housewives off with their spare saucepans, leaving them with reduced equipment. A brilliantly successful propaganda exercise, the campaign was otherwise of little practical value. The quality of the metal handed in was simply not good enough to make aircraft with.

The best way to improve food supplies was to grow or rear it oneself. Land previously left to waste was brought into cultivation, including public parks and railway embankments. This was the celebrated 'Dig for Victory' campaign, which popularised the allotment system across Britain. Farmland was also extended, some 4 million hectares (10 million acres) of grassland alone being ploughed up, which required a vast investment in machinery. Farmers who proved unwilling or unable to respond to the demands being made on them were liable to find themselves summarily evicted – a ruthless side of the

Spitfire II P8441 on display in Gravesend, Kent, in spring 1943 to raise funds, in the markings of No. 277 Squadron.

Above left: *A Government poster links a full plate with home gardening.*

Above right: *The 'Dig for Victory' campaign is exploited by a business to advertise its own gardening products.*

nation at war, which is easily forgotten. Much of the extra work was undertaken by the Women's Land Army.

As a result of this process, Britain's dependence on imported foods dropped to around one-third of her needs. Potatoes and carrots were comparatively abundant as a result, despite their lack of immediate popularity as relentless daily features. The roast chicken was once an occasional treat. During the war it became a scarce luxury unless there was room to accommodate chickens in the garden along with rabbits, and this practice became increasingly common.

The psychological effects of food shortages were not forgotten. The occasional availability of modest indulgences eased the sensation of nutritional gloom symbolised by the indigestible 'National Wheatmeal Loaf'.

This poster made the Women's Land Army seem positively romantic. But it was also extremely hard work.

In the Home Front, a modest luxury such as this tiny bar of ration chocolate could play a significant part in morale.

Rationing was modified to a points system, which allowed a self-selected allocation of allowances among a range of goods. The arrival of American forces in Britain did much to renew a sense of promise. Often welcomed for overwhelming generosity, US troops took time out to donate foods and treats, particularly to local children. Food parcels also arrived from across the Atlantic, which by 1943 was becoming safer. Nevertheless, the shortages would remain long after the war.

Against a scene of Blitz devastation, Home Front stomachs are kept full by an Allied Relief Fund van distributing essentials raised by charity in the United States for Britain's bomb victims.

American troops share their afternoon tea with British civilians, who often delighted in their generosity and informality.

Normal life carried on. These advertisements promoted knitting, cold cures, games and boilers.

PERSONAL EFFECTS

Nowadays, cheap clothing is abundant and high-street shops creak under the weight of stocks of deodorants, cosmetics and personal-grooming goods. Many of these would have been incomprehensible indulgences before the war, let alone during it. During the war, even the basic hygiene priorities of the 1930s took second place to more pressing requirements. With baths restricted to a depth of 13 cm (5 inches), the Home Front family member also had to choose between body soap or washing powder from his or her ration allocation. Razor blades became virtually unobtainable and had to be sharpened by running them over glass.

PUT OUT YOUR PAPER
FOR SALVAGE

Left: No chance was missed to promote recycling.

Below: Looking good was considered essential to morale, though limited coupon allocations inspired ingenuity.

6 Home Front FASHIONS
(WOMEN, CHILDREN & MEN)

WITH SMART FINISHING TOUCHES VIA YOUR SEWING MACHINE

FREE PAPER PATTERN / *Choose any design inside.* SEE PAGES 1.16
(VALUE 6d)

Below: Models turn out to display the range of styles that could still be made in a time of chronic shortage.

Clothes rationing began in mid 1941. Imported clothes were unobtainable and factories that had produced civilian clothing went over to manufacturing uniforms or other war equipment. At twenty-six coupons, a man's suit could use up nearly half the year's allocation, while a woman's frock and a pair of stockings took nine. A complete outfit, including underwear, for a man or a woman could clean out the allowance in an instant. In later years, rationing was increased and, together with steadily rising prices, caused the introduction of economical 'utility' clothing. Made to standard designs from specified materials, utility clothing was often resented for being drab but it gained widespread acceptance for making the best of a bad job.

The austerity of the Depression made good practice for the Home Front.

Inevitably, the Home Front household resorted to make do and mend, with endless recycling of curtains and bedspreads into dresses and other items, though the background of the Depression meant that these were already well-practised activities. Sock-darning, now almost a lost art, was routine, as were the repair of fraying trousers and the unravelling of wool to turn an adult's worn sweater into a child's.

In an age when tobacco consumption has declined in popularity, the dependence of the 1940s adult on cigarettes is difficult to appreciate. It seemed that many people were more willing to queue for cigarettes than for anything else, only to find themselves with a highly restricted choice of brands. At one stage in the war, women were officially exhorted to desist from smoking so that men could have first call on supplies. Tobacco inevitably featured in the black market as a result. But with Winston Churchill's cigar smoking playing such a prominent part in his image, the government had to do what it could to maintain supplies.

This magazine cover reinforces the importance of domestic pride, while the subtle photograph of an airman boyfriend or husband links the role to the war effort.

This poster called women forward to help with evacuated children by working for the WVS (Women's Voluntary Service).

GOING TO WORK

The war brought unprecedented demands for arms and equipment. Not only that, but the Battle of the Atlantic meant most would have to be made in Britain. The workforce had to be maximised and factories abandoned peacetime products. Many joiners, for example, found themselves making De Havilland Mosquito wooden fighter-bombers. Women would have to work too. The First World War set a precedent, with many women working in munitions factories and leading to the social revolution in women's rights in the inter-war years. Voluntary work was of vital importance. The Women's Voluntary Service was begun in 1938, as part of the lead-up to war, in the hope that women could be integrated into ARP work from the outset. It was dramatically successful, and the WVS badge became as familiar as the ARP badge in the Home Front, as the women ran rest centres, bomb-site field kitchens, nurseries and even mobile laundries, though occasionally they were seen by some as rather too authoritarian for their own good.

A woman assembles part of a Spitfire's fuselage.

Britain lost vast quantities of material at Dunkirk and needed to produce more equipment for the army. Aircraft absorbed enormous amounts of effort. A single four-engine Lancaster bomber built from 1942 was an extremely complex machine but was eventually produced at a rate of one per hour. By 1941, the need for labour was increasing in urgency. Advertisements appeared across Britain for women to work, leading to the conscription of women into the armed forces or industry by the end of the year. In 1943, some men conscripted into the forces were diverted into the mines to make good a steady decline in production – the so-called 'Bevin Boys', most of whom profoundly resented the imposition.

Women in the forces did not fight but they played vital roles in civil defence, intelligence, administration and catering. Women in industry worked on everything from the production of domestic goods to manufacturing barrage balloons and welding components of heavy bombers. The Women's Land Army, finally numbering some 80,000, dispatched women across the country to work on farms, though they were subsequently assisted by prisoners of war. Around 100,000 women took jobs on the railways, while others worked in demolition gangs, as pipe-layers, household-equipment installation engineers or, indeed, practically anything.

At the time this was radical – it was generally expected that married women in particular would stay at home, even if they had no children, while many young single women might have gone into service and were delighted to find that there was more to life than cleaning fire grates for the kind of affluent young women who expected never to have to work at all. The call-up

BITS OF CARELESS TALK
ARE PIECED TOGETHER BY THE ENEMY

Convoy sails for England tonight

Workplaces, and the journey to work, were perfect places for spies to overhear conversations.

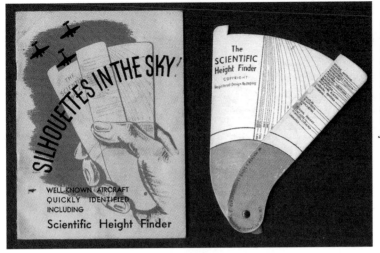

One of the numerous devices manufactured that reflected how exciting life on the Home Front seemed, especially to the young.

created a crisis in the labour market for maids and cooks. There was also a residual concern that women at work would end up taking jobs from men once the war was over.

But there were psychological advantages, as well as moral pressure. For a woman at home, with her husband away with the armed services, loneliness was swiftly dispatched with a job,

especially if the work was linked to her husband's role. Some women, whose child-care responsibilities would have exempted them, campaigned for Government-financed nurseries so that they could contribute to a job, exclaiming 'Nurseries for Kids! War Work for Mothers!' An affluent young woman, launched into high society in 1939 and fully expecting a life of parties and a successful marriage, might find herself labouring in an aircraft factory by 1942. She discovered not only her own capacity for hard work and skills, but a world that she scarcely knew existed. The war was a great social leveller.

The overall result was that the majority of adult women under the age of forty spent 1941–5 at work, with women up to fifty years old being

Long hours in difficult conditions left factory workers exhausted, but a sense of purpose often kept them going.

This composed publicity shot makes no reference to the hard labour, driving rain, winter snow and barren living conditions endured by women on farms.

brought in from 1943. The conditions that were tolerated would lead to riots today. Many people worked shifts lasting more than twelve hours, seven days a week, while living in hostels. The Land Army, for example, enjoyed one week's holiday a year. Exhausted workers were susceptible to diseases like tuberculosis. For all this, women were expected to work for significantly lower wages than their male colleagues. Those with families struggled to hold down jobs while also running homes. But the sense of purpose generally proved more pervasive, in spite of occasional strikes. Enthusiasm to be seen pulling one's weight overcame the hardships.

A Heinkel He111 bomber lies wrecked amongst the ruins of a house in Clacton, Essex, having been shot down by anti-aircraft fire on 30th April 1940. Two civilians were killed and more than 150 injured.

TRAVEL

Today, we take it for granted that we can move about at will but during the war the question 'Is Your Journey Really Necessary?' screamed at the public from Government posters. Before 1939, car ownership was still restricted to the relatively affluent. Car factories were rapidly turned over to war production. Petrol rationing limited the use of existing cars to at most 200 miles (320 km) a month, with more for essential users. It was hardly surprising. A squadron of twelve Spitfires that took off for each sortie needed more than 1000 gallons (4500 litres) of petrol between them, equivalent to the ration for an Austin Seven for twenty-one years!

Petrol rationing quickly led to a black market in fuel designated for commercial or official use, despite the fact that it was dyed red and could make 32.5 pence (6s 6d) a gallon, four times as much as legitimate supplies. Those less inclined to buy illegal petrol tried adding paraffin to the petrol tank, with variable results – usually a lot more noise and smell. But owning a car was academic after March 1942, when petrol was completely withdrawn from private use. Cars generally went on blocks in garages and stayed there until 1945.

Actually finding one's way around the country became a nightmare. The black-out would have made road signs unreadable, had they not already been removed along with milestones. At strategic locations, road blocks made of concrete

This poster advised the driver on the dimmed lights and painted matt-white stripes to be used in the black-out. However, accidents were frequent and numerous.

Dover Castle, Kent, overlooks a bombed street where the town's bus drivers stolidly maintained the service, as others did across Britain.

slabs, or even tar barrels, narrowed roads so that traffic could be forced through checkpoints. Here drivers were asked to explain their reasons for being out. An unnecessary car journey – even a non-essential short diversion from an otherwise vital journey – could result in a prison sentence or at least a very substantial fine. The idea was to save fuel and confound the plans of any would-be invaders. As the invasion never came, the result was no more than years of inconvenience.

Instead, people relied on bicycles, buses, trains and hitching lifts. Basic deliveries continued to be made by horse and cart. Rail, above all else, was the mass transportation service of the conflict. From the outbreak of war, the Government took over the regional rail companies. Vast numbers of trains were laid on to move troops about, to freight equipment and to shift Blitz debris, while 'normal services' were heavily reduced. Blacked-out carriages rendered night-time journeys unutterably tedious, and painted-out or removed station signs confounded attempts to track one's route. Carriages were packed and even lavatories filled with passengers. Seats were hard to get, and most people resigned themselves to endless hours of standing in corridors. London's underground system was less affected – the black-out, for instance, scarcely applied – but passengers had to find their way around members of the public sheltering from raids.

Railways were the backbone of Britain's wartime transport, but troops took priority. This train has been commandeered from normal service to transport soldiers evacuated from Dunkirk in May 1940.

Members of the Home Guard parade through Sevenoaks, Kent, in August 1941.

THE HOME GUARD

Although the Government made highly secret preparations for a German invasion, including building subterranean cells packed with equipment for a resistance movement, the public face of civilian defence was the Local Defence Volunteers, or the Home Guard. Forever enshrined in the popular BBC comedy series *Dad's Army*, the Home Guard began in May 1940 when civilian men between the ages of seventeen and sixty-five were asked to join up.

The willing volunteers had to make do with a motley collection of uniforms and equipment, arming themselves with ancient rifles trawled from museums, farms and private collectors. Even bayonets tied onto pipes served for a while. Eventually, around two million men had signed up and took part in drill, weapons practice and military exercises. The idea was that the Home Guard would confront German invaders in the streets. For the most part, though, Home Guard work involved tedious manning of look-outs

High-tech defences. The original caption to this picture, published in 1940, says 'A number of pigeon fanciers have joined the Home Guard in a North-west area where large stretches of moorland have to be watched and patrolled. The men use their pigeons to act as messengers between the outposts and headquarters.'

and guns. Individual experiences varied enormously, depending often on how seriously the 'officers' took their roles and exercised their authority.

The Home Guard did not see out the war. In November 1944 it was disbanded. Any prospect of a German invasion had long since waned. Perhaps it was just as well. When the Allies thundered across Germany in 1945 they, too, found an army increasingly made up of elderly men and boys, and which offered them little effective resistance.

The wreckage of a Messerschmitt Bf109 fighter in Welling, Kent, after it crashed there on 20th October 1940. Controlling crowds and preventing souvenir hunting were some of the duties fulfilled by the Home Guard.

EVACUATION

Of all the images of the Home Front, that of children gathered together on railway platforms clutching bags and gas masks is the most enduring. Practice evacuations started in June 1939. Seen as the practical solution to protecting children from bombs, evacuation was an intensely variable experience. Parents suffered a form of bereavement when their children left, while the children found themselves propelled into the unknown. The other side of the coin was that while evacuation was voluntary, having evacuees billeted on one was compulsory.

Normally, evacuated children travelled with their schoolteachers. Otherwise, women responded to posters seeking volunteers to come and help with shepherding the children into trains and seeing them to their new homes. Packed off on trains to remote locations, many had to endure the humiliating experience of standing in church halls clutching their belongings while local people selected children they liked the look of. The cruelty of this randomness reached its climax when siblings were split up – some families preferring to take their chances with demure-looking small girls and rejecting their older brothers. Once the children had been billeted, cards were filled in with their new address and sent to their parents.

In other cases, boarding schools relocated *en masse*, which at

Children set off with excited expressions to their new wartime homes. Some had wonderful times, but others found misery.

People in the countryside were reminded of their responsibility to care for those whose lives had been destroyed in the bombardment of cities.

It might be YOU!

CARING FOR EVACUEES IS A NATIONAL SERVICE

least allowed stability of a sort. Sometimes, evacuation was arranged on an individual basis but it was not until the middle of 1940 that any official financial help was provided for those with small children who did this. The result was, as usual, that the better off had more options than the rest of the population.

By January 1940, long before the Blitz began, many children had been returned to their homes, though some were later sent away again. The opportunity to be sent to the other side of the world came in June 1940, when overseas evacuation to British dominions was arranged, though wealthier families with relatives or friends abroad were already sending their children away. It seemed sensible but Churchill denounced as thoroughly unpatriotic the haste with which some families rushed to apply for places. The dangers became all too apparent when an evacuee ship was sunk by a U-boat torpedo. More than seventy children were killed, and the plan was abandoned.

Those who remained in the countryside experienced everything from real happiness to utter misery, depending on where they were billeted. Urban working-class children, more accustomed to swearing and fighting, horrified rural snobs who saw them as corrupting influences on their own offspring. In the worst cases, beatings and even sexual abuse followed. Evacuation did not even guarantee safety from the war. In May 1942, for example, an air raid destroyed houses in Exeter, to which children had been evacuated.

Commercial survival led some companies to relocate to the countryside or cities as far away as possible from the threat of attack. Employees found themselves being presented with the choice of moving or resigning, while married couples faced separation when either or both were told their companies were moving.

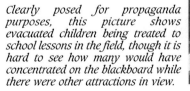

Clearly posed for propaganda purposes, this picture shows evacuated children being treated to school lessons in the field, though it is hard to see how many would have concentrated on the blackboard while there were other attractions in view.

ENTERTAINMENT

By 1939, cinema had become the main form of visual entertainment while the radio ruled the home and the workplace, where shows like *Music While You Work* helped offset drudgery. The impact of American popular music had already been felt before the war in the black-and-white musical films, such as *Dames*, of the mid 1930s. British singers like Al Bowlly were immensely popular, as were American bands, for example Glenn Miller's US Army Air Force band. Both men were killed during the war, adding to the poignancy of the time in which they made their reputations. American influence steadily increased through popular song. Judy Garland's 'Somewhere over the Rainbow', for example, from *The Wizard of Oz*, and Vera Lynn's 'It's a Lovely Day Tomorrow', became anthems for hope and nostalgia.

Britain produced a variety of celebrated movies to keep the Home Front rallied. Stirring films such as *In Which We Serve* (1942) brought the military world and Home Front together. In one memorable scene, the Blitz leads to the destruction of a house in which two naval wives are staying. One is killed, and the other writes to her husband on board ship, leaving him to tell his shipmate the terrible news. Such fictional tragedies mirrored the reality of the random fate of war and emphasised the shared risk of husbands and wives, wherever they were. *Henry V* was a subtler attempt at stimulating a sense of national purpose and pride. Colour sensations from Hollywood such as *Gone with the Wind* attracted vast audiences, who often proved unmovable when air-raid sirens sounded. In its escapist historical setting, but

Cinemas were centres of public information as well as of entertainment.

Below: *Entertainment the Nazi way. After the Channel Islands fell to the Germans in 1940, a cinema gave the 'lucky' locals the chance to watch a Nazi propaganda film, 'Sieg im Westen' ('Victory in the West').*

Above left: *This sheet music, printed in England in 1942, provided the home or pub pianist with the music for the Gordon–Warren song 'Serenade in Blue', played by Glenn Miller and his orchestra in the Hollywood motion picture 'Orchestra Wives'.*

Above right: *While cinema was the centre of public entertainment, radio ruled the home and workplace in the Home Front.*

Below: *At New Cross Stadium, south London, on 29th July 1943, the Deptford Beautification and Social Affairs Committee arranged family sports and activities, including this merry-go-round, to break the sense of monotonous deprivation.*

with the all-too-reminiscent backdrop of the Civil War and the burning of Atlanta, the movie was intoxicating and beguiling.

A different, but predictable, pastime was sex. Despite the cinema portrayal of the stoic British family at war, the Home Front also saw an explosion in prostitution and casual encounters. The black-out and the unavoidable 'here today, gone tomorrow' mood of war collapsed inhibitions. But British society's natural tendency to prudery was even more pronounced in the 1940s. There was official reluctance to acknowledge problems like venereal disease, and to provide medical facilities. During 1942, it was claimed, more people suffered from venereal disease than had been casualties in the Blitz in 1941. Not until October 1942 did a proper Government campaign begin.

For women, going to work (often for the first time) was also a social experience. For women whose husbands were away fighting, it was not always easy to resist the temptation to 'drift', as it was called. Male colleagues, British, Dominion or US troops billeted nearby – all offered the prospect of companionship and relationships. Casual prostitution was rife compared to peacetime. After the war there was a substantial increase in the divorce rate, mostly on grounds of adultery.

American Army Air Force personnel dance the night away with British women invited to the base for an evening's entertainment. The women will have spent hours making themselves look as glamorous as possible with what they had to hand.

CONCLUSION

The defeat of Germany in May 1945, and the fall of Japan a few months later in August, might have brought to an end the fighting, but the Home Front remained. Rationing was to last until well into the 1950s. Shortages of just about everything were compounded by Britain's desperate need to pay for the war. Manufactured goods were often designated 'export only', and imported goods were rare. Homes and families had to readjust to the return of their menfolk. Others faced a future in which vital family members were never to return.

The end of the war brought great relief, but also a sudden disappearance of purpose. For nearly six years, the war had provided an underlying dynamic to life, provoking myriad examples of private and personal heroism, dedication and unselfishness. With that purpose, good or ill, gone, there was a profound sense of anticlimax for some people. Looking back, more than half a century later, it is not difficult to feel a pang of envy for an age with a quality of spirit. Reviewing Channel 4's *1940s House*, a television programme recreating Home Front life, the journalist Charlotte Raven observed that the war years were 'the one time in modern British history when goodness and nobility brought more rewards than selfishness and greed'.

Prefabricated housing was one quick way of rehousing bombed-out families and made use of redundant factories after the war was over. These examples were still in use in Eltham, south-east London, in the early twenty-first century.

FURTHER READING

Second-hand bookshops, junk shops and jumble sales are ideal places to scour for wartime newspapers, books and pamphlets. Many of the items featured in this book were found in such places. These items make ideal teaching aids, while it can be fun to make recipes from contemporary cookery books.

The *1940s Historical Society* is one of many Internet resources and can be found at www.1940.co.uk

Brown, M., and Harris, C. *The Wartime House*. Sutton Publishing, 2001.
Gardiner, J. *The 1940s House*. Channel 4 Books, 2000.
Hylton, S. *Their Darkest Hour*. Sutton Publishing, 2000.
Lewis, P. *A People's War*. Thames Methuen, 1986.
Longmate, N. *How We Lived Then: A History of Everyday Life during the Second World War*. Arrow Books, 1973.
Patten, M. *We'll Eat Again*. Hamlyn, 1985.
Perry, C. *The Boy in the Blitz*. Colin Perry, 1980.
Ramsey, W.G. (editor). *The Blitz Then and Now: Volume 1, September 3, 1939–September 6, 1940*. After the Battle Magazine, 1987.
Ramsey, W.G. (editor). *The Blitz Then and Now: Volume 2, September 7, 1940–May 1941*. After the Battle Magazine, 1989.
Ramsey, W.G. (editor). *The Blitz Then and Now: Volume 3, May 1941–May 1945*. After the Battle Magazine, 1990.

PLACES TO VISIT

It is always advisable to telephone in advance to check opening arrangements and to find out whether the galleries or displays you wish to see are accessible. The following is only a small selection. Almost every city, town or village museum in the British Isles includes a selection of items from the Home Front, often featuring details of local industries, as well as domestic items.

Britain at War Experience, 64–66 Tooley Street, London Bridge, London SE1 2TF. Telephone: 020 7403 3171. Website: www.britainatwar.co.uk
Cabinet War Rooms, Clive Steps, King Charles Street, London SW1A 2AQ. Telephone: 020 7930 6961. Website: www.iwm.org.uk/cabinet/index.htm
Derby Industrial Museum, Full Street, Derby DE1 3AF. Telephone: 01332 255308. Website: www.derby.gov.uk/museums
Eden Camp, Malton, North Yorkshire YO17 6RT. Telephone: 01653 697777. Website: www.edencamp.co.uk
Geffrye Museum, Kingsland Road, London E2 8EA. Telephone: 020 7739 9893. Website: www.geffrye-museum.org.uk
Imperial War Museum, Lambeth Road, London SE1 6HZ. Telephone: 020 7416 5320. Website: www.iwm.org.uk
Museum of Kent Life, Cobtree, Lock Lane, Sandling, Maidstone, Kent ME14 3AU. Telephone: 01622 763936. Website: www.museum-kentlife.co.uk
York Castle Museum, Eye of York, York YO1 9RY. Telephone: 01904 687687. Website: www.yorkcastlemuseum.org.uk